The Heart of the Matter:

Effects of Catholic High Schools on Student Values, Beliefs and Behaviors

Authors:
Michael J. Guerra
Michael J. Donahue
Peter L. Benson

A Project of the
NATIONAL CATHOLIC EDUCATIONAL ASSOCIATION

In Collaboration with
SEARCH INSTITUTE

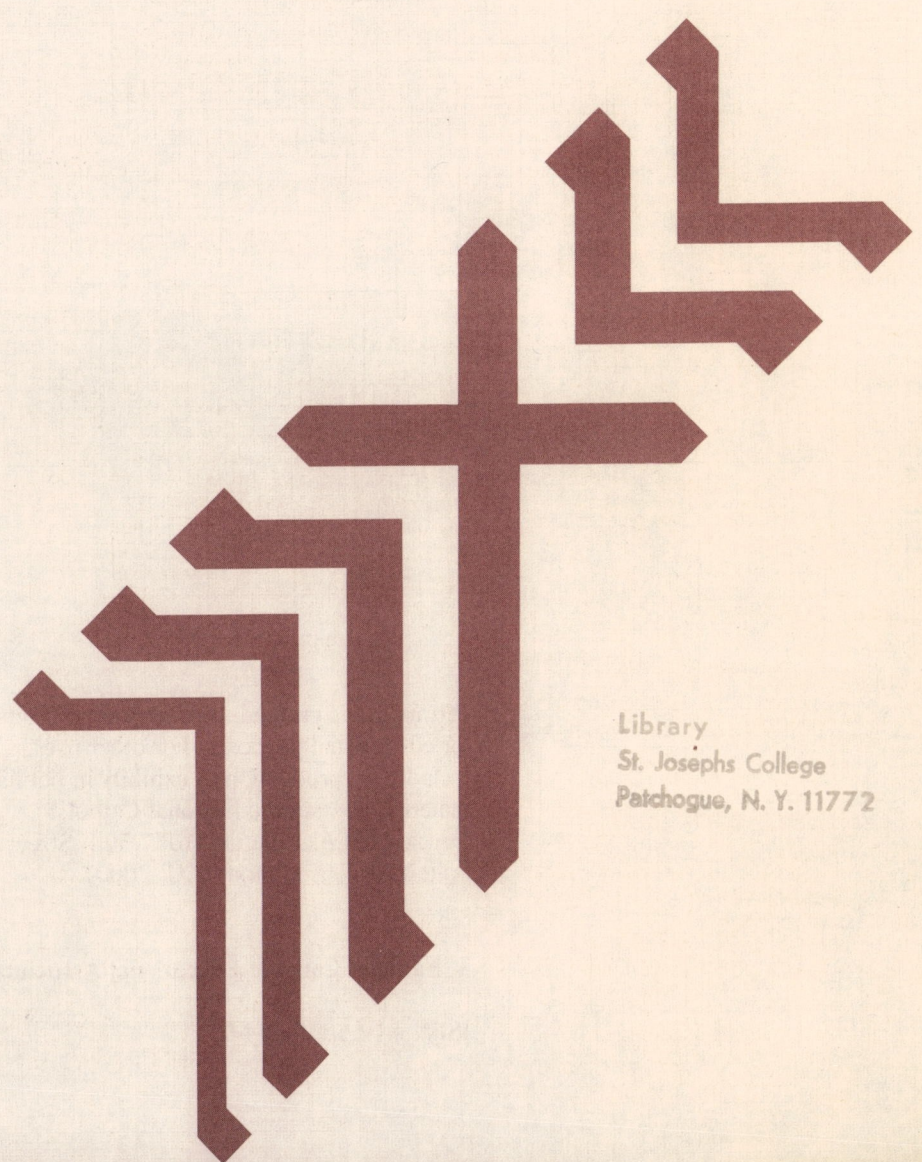

© National Catholic Educational Association, 1990

ISBN #1-55833-044-5

Table of Contents

ACKNOWLEDGMENTS   vii

OVERVIEW AND HIGHLIGHTS   ix

CHAPTER 1
INTRODUCTION   1

CHAPTER 2
The Effects of Catholic High Schools on Students   3
A SUMMARY OF CURRENT RESEARCH ON
ACADEMIC IMPACTS

   High School and Beyond   3
      Academic Achievement   3
      Low Income and Minority Student Achievement   4
      College Attendance and Achievement   4
      Dropout and Retention Rates   4

   Other National Studies   4

   Explanations for Academic Effectiveness   6
      School Climate   6
      Parental Involvement   8
      Teacher Commitment   8
      Leadership and Autonomy   9
      Academic Curriculum   10
      The School and the Functional Community   10

CHAPTER 3
The Effects of Catholic High Schools on Students   13
VALUES, BELIEFS, AND BEHAVIORS

   Previous Research on Non-Academic Outcomes   14
      Convey   14
      Greeley   14
      NCEA   15
      Summary   16

The Present Study   16
    Where the Data Come From   16

Methodology   17
    The Data Set   17
    Background and Outcome Variables   17

Descriptive Statistics   20
    The Current Picture   20
        Family and Personal Background   20
        Outcome Measures   20
        Summary   22
    Ten Year Trends   22
        Family and Personal Background   23
        Social Values   25
        Educational Values   25
        Concern for People   25
        At-Risk Behaviors   26
        Perceptions of Self   26
        Faith and Church   26
        Summary   26

Determinants of Outcomes: What "Causes" the Differences?   27
    Methodology   27
    Social Values   27
    Educational Values   29
    Concern for People   29
    At-Risk Behaviors   30
    Perceptions of Self   30
    Faith and Church   30
    Summary   30

CHAPTER 4
SUMMARY AND CONCLUSIONS   33

Initial Thoughts   33
    Differences between Groups   33
    Ten-Year Trends   33
    Determinants of Outcomes   34

School Effects   34
    Social Values   34
    Educational Values   34
    Concern for People   35
    At-Risk Behaviors   35
    Perceptions of Self   35
    Faith and Church   36
    A Model of Catholic High School Effects   36

Final Thoughts   38

The Authors

Michael J. Guerra, the project director, is Executive Director, Secondary School Department, National Catholic Educational Association, Washington, DC.

Michael J. Donahue, the principal investigator, is Chief Research Scientist at Search Institute.

Peter L. Benson, associate project director, is President of Search Institute, Minneapolis, MN.

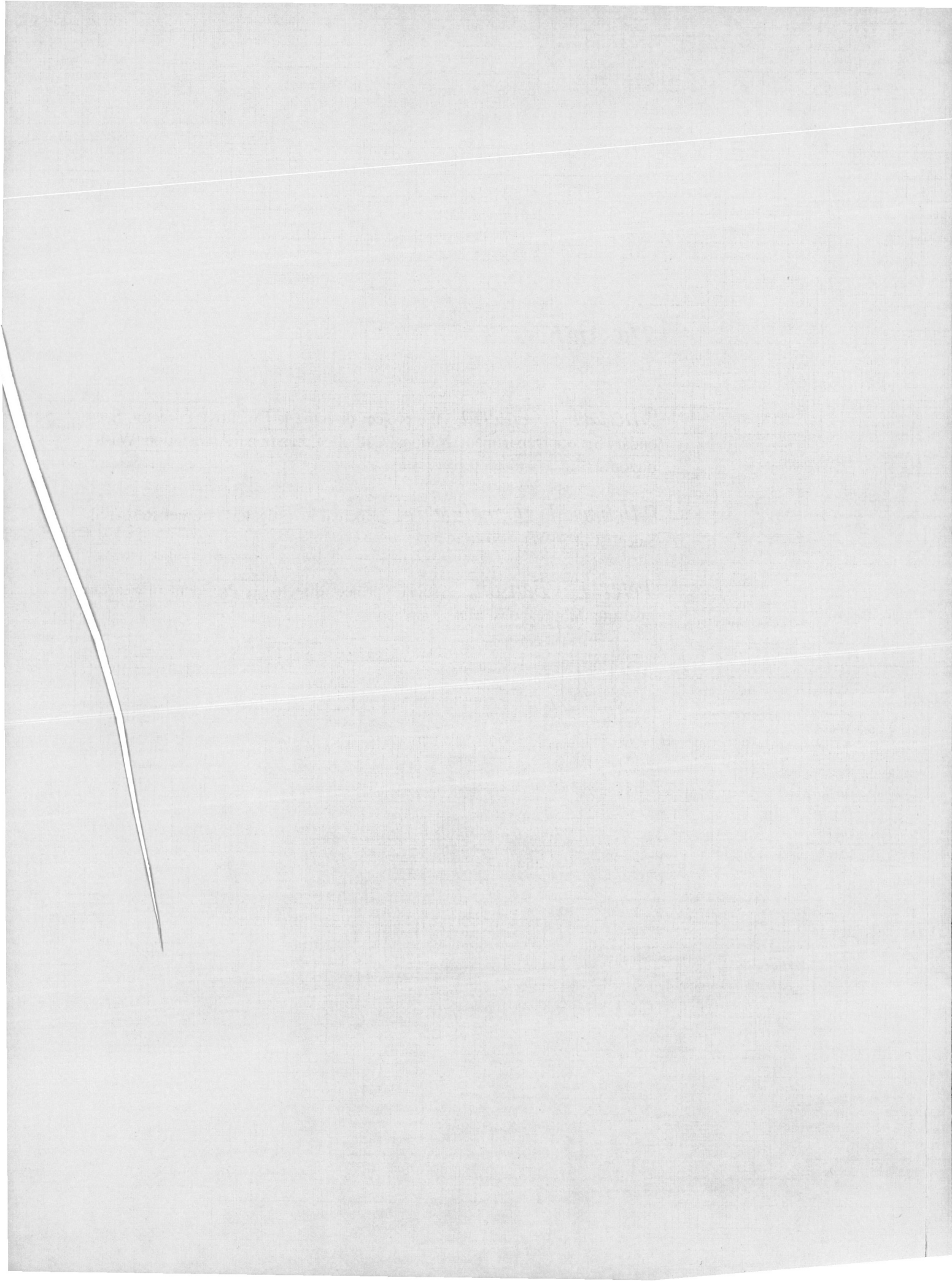

Acknowledgements

The Heart of the Matter: Effects of Catholic High Schools on Student Values, Beliefs and Behaviors describes a project that began in 1986. The authors of this report are indebted to a great many people whose contributions at various stages have been invaluable to the project.

Funding for this project was provided by matching grants from the St. Marys Foundation and the Father Michael J. McGivney Fund for New Initiatives in Catholic Education.

The summaries of other relevant studies which appear in chapter 2 and the first part of chapter 3 include materials from major presentations by Michael Guerra (Denver, September 1988) and Peter Benson (Chicago, April 1989). The original design and statistical analyses of the new data set drawn from the *Monitoring the Future* project were developed by Michael Donahue, the project's principal investigator.

We invited a number of our colleagues to review and critique preliminary drafts of this report. We are indebted to Brother Milton Barker, FSC, Superintendent, Totino-Grace High School, Fridley, MN; Dr. George Elford, Educational Testing Service, Washington, DC; Brother Marcellin Flynn, FMS, St. Joseph's College, Australia; Brother John McGovern, CSC, Superintendent of Schools, Archdiocese of Hartford, CT; Dr. Bernard Spilka, Department of Psychology, University of Denver; Sister Mary Peter Traviss, OP, Institute of Catholic Educational Leadership, University of San Francisco; and Dr. Herbert Walberg, Research Professor of Urban Affairs, University of Illinois at Chicago.

At the National Catholic Educational Association, Denise Eggers provided editorial assistance and guided the manuscript through the various stages of production.

The Heart of the Matter is the fourth in a series of research reports produced by NCEA's Secondary School Department in collaboration with Search Institute. Earlier studies published by the Secondary School Department include *The Catholic High School: A National Portrait* (1985); *Catholic High Schools: Their Impact on Low-Income Students* (1986); and *Sharing the Faith: The Beliefs and Values of Catholic High School Teachers* (1985).

While we do not claim that these and other studies described in this report exhaust the possibilities for significant research, we believe that our work has contributed to an important and growing body of research examining the effectiveness of Catholic schools. As we review the evidence, we become increasingly convinced that Catholic schools, while hardly perfect, are powerful and positive instruments in shaping the academic and spiritual growth of their students. For a nation straining to find ways to educate all of its children, Catholic schools represent important models of academic success. For a society struggling to find ways to build a community of compassion and justice, Catholic schools represent unique and invaluable resources. For a church committed to sharing its faith and its future with succeeding generations, Catholic schools represent a strong and perhaps indispensable source of continuity and renewal. We are encouraged by what we have learned about Catholic schools, and we trust this report may contribute to increased understanding and appreciation for the contributions that these schools make to the intellectual, civic and spiritual health of the Catholic community and the nation at large.

Michael J. Guerra
Project Director
Washington, DC
The Feast of the Epiphany, 1990

Overview and Highlights

This report begins with a review of the literature concerning the effectiveness of Catholic high schools. It then presents new information based on an analysis of the annual, nationwide *Monitoring the Future* survey of high school seniors. The analysis of this survey examines differences between Catholic seniors attending Catholic high schools and those enrolled in public high schools in the areas of social values, educational values, concern for people, at-risk behaviors, perceptions of self, and religiousness. Beginning with a descriptive portrait, the report goes on to examine gender differences, school differences, and ten-year trends in the responses of seniors in Catholic high schools. The report concludes with a discussion of the independent effects of various background variables and schooling on a variety of non-academic outcome variables. It finds that Catholic schooling, over and above other factors, has a significant and positive effect on student attitudes about militarism, marriage, educational aspiration, likelihood of cutting school, concern for others, frequency of church attendance, and the importance of religion. Catholic high school seniors were found to have somewhat less positive attitudes toward school, an effect the authors suggest may be attributed to more rigorous academic demands in Catholic high schools. Other major influences on outcome variables are the perceived importance of religion, and the number of nights per week the student goes out for "fun and recreation." The report concludes with a discussion of possible explanations for these differences.

CHAPTER 1

Introduction

During the last seven years a widespread concern about American education has turned educational research into a growth industry. Spurred on by calls for reform in American education (e.g., *A Nation at Risk*, 1983; *What Works*, 1986), a plethora of studies examined how, when, and why some schools are effective and some are ineffective. Much of this research has been particularly encouraging to the Catholic educational community. In virtually every study that compares students in Catholic and public schools, the students in Catholic schools display levels of academic achievement that are substantially higher than their counterparts in public schools, even after family background differences between the two groups of students have been statistically controlled.

While such studies are potentially useful, not only to Catholic educators but to all who are interested in identifying the elements that determine the academic effectiveness of schools, they present a manifestly incomplete picture of Catholic schools. The mission of Catholic schools includes more than the promotion of learning in the traditional academic sense. Catholic schools also care about their students' faith , their commitment to the Church, their values, and their present and future lifestyles. To fully describe the effectiveness of Catholic schools, research attention has to be paid to important "non-academic" outcomes. The research concerning such outcomes is relatively modest; a brief review of some important earlier studies in this area is presented in Chapter 3. But now a new national study of Catholic high school seniors helps extend our knowledge of Catholic school impact beyond the academic arena to behaviors and values. This new information, when combined with earlier outcome studies, suggests that Catholic high schools excel in *both* the academic and non-academic domains.

The purpose of this report is to present the full picture of Catholic high school impact, first by synthesizing the research on academic outcomes, and then by presenting what has recently been learned about behavior and value outcomes.

A Summary of Current Research on Academic Impact

High School and Beyond

The most rigorous and comprehensive studies of school effects are based on analyses of the data generated by a series of surveys entitled *High School and Beyond* (e.g., Coleman and Hoffer, 1987; Coleman, Hoffer, and Kilgore, 1982). Funded by the U.S. Department of Education and begun in 1980, this study tracks the academic progress of 30,000 individuals who were high school sophomores in 1980. These students, including representative samples of both public school and Catholic school sophomores, have been surveyed at two-year intervals. The longitudinal design of this study helps to insure that differences over time are not due to differences between the people involved in the study, since the same group of people (as nearly as possible) is involved each year. Four important findings emerge from analyses of this pioneering research, and each speaks to the favorable academic impact of Catholic schools.

Academic Achievement

Like much of the research in this area, the *High School and Beyond* study measures academic achievement through the use of standardized tests in the areas of reading, vocabulary, mathematics, science and civics. These tests have their shortcomings, but they do provide some insights about what students know and how their knowledge changes over time.

Achievement tests were administered to high school sophomores and seniors in the 1980 *High School and Beyond* data collection. Coleman et al. (1982) reported that for every subject area tested, the average student in Catholic and other private schools scored above the average student in public high schools.

Such differences could be due, in part, to differences between public and private school students in family background and socioeconomic status. In their reexamination of the effects of school type on achievement, Coleman and Hoffer (1987) used the 1980 and 1982 *High School and Beyond* longitudinal data set to compare achievement growth between the sophomore and senior years in public, Catholic and other private schools. In their analysis, the authors controlled statistically for the differences in family and social background. These controls included race, socio-economic status, region, handicap status, the student's college plans in 9th grade, and parents' educational aspirations for their child.

Even with these controls, Coleman and Hoffer (1987) report that significant differences between the academic achievements of public high school students and Catholic high school students remain. Catholic high school students, compared with public high school students, gain more in four of the six tested areas: reading, vocabulary, mathematics, and writing. In two other areas, civics and science, achievement growth does not differ between Catholic high school students and public high school students. When comparing non-Catholic private schools to public schools, significantly greater growth is observed in only two of the six areas (reading and writing).

Low Income and Minority Student Achievement

The positive effect of Catholic schools on academic achievement is particularly pronounced for low-income and minority students (cf. Benson et al., 1986; Greeley, 1982). In public high schools, the achievement gap between low-income and other students tends to widen during the high school years. In Catholic high schools, low-income youth gain as much academically as do other students. One reason for this is that in Catholic high schools, almost all students are expected to pursue a rigorous academic program. Seventy percent of low-income students are in an academic track, 88% take four years of English during high school, and 67% take three years of mathematics. These are impressive figures, exceeding by a wide margin what the average public high school student takes during the high school years.

College Attendance and Achievement

Eighty-three percent of Catholic high school graduates in 1982 entered a college or university, compared with 52% of public high school graduates. Of those high school graduates attending college, Catholic high school students are more likely to remain in college and matriculate with a baccalaureate degree than are public high school students. Black and Hispanic Catholic high school graduates in the class of 1982 are three times more likely to have earned a degree by 1986 than Black and Hispanic public high school graduates.

Dropout and Retention Rates

Catholic high schools are much more successful in preventing school dropout than public or other private schools. The dropout rate of 1980 high school sophomores between the spring of the sophomore year and spring of the senior year was 3.4% in Catholic high schools, 11.9% in other private schools, and 14.4% in public high schools.

Other National Studies

Other national studies, though controlling less rigorously for background differences, provide additional evidence about the academic performance of Catholic school students. In the school year 1983-84 the National Assessment of Educational Progress assessed reading proficiency on a national sample of

FIGURE 1: Percentage of 1980 high school sophomores dropping out of school between spring of sophomore year and spring of senior year, by high school type

Percent

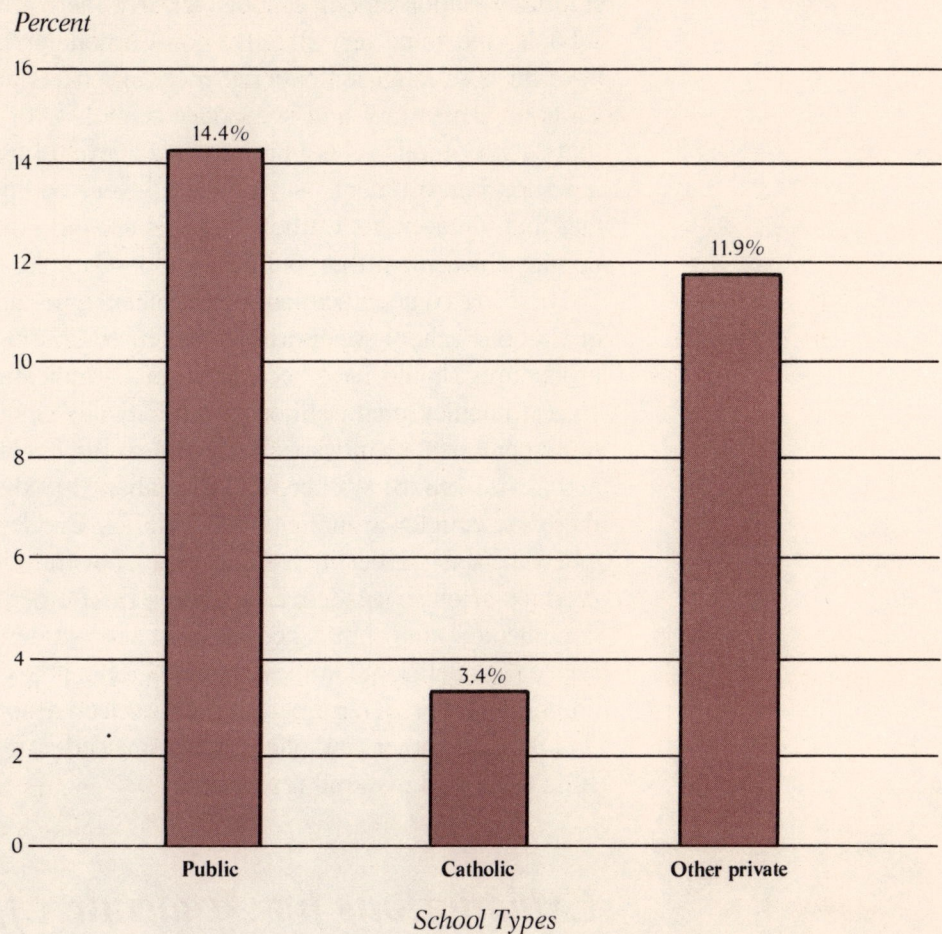

School Types

SOURCE: Coleman, J. & Hoffer, T. (1987). *Public and Private Schools: The Impact of Communities.* New York: Basic Books, p. 99.

20,000 students in each of three grades: 4, 8, and 11. About 2000 Catholic school students were included from each grade. At each grade level, Catholic school students out-scored the rest of the nation. These differences held when comparing Catholic and public school subgroups by gender and race. In every case, Catholic school students in all three grade levels out-scored their public high school counterparts (Lee, 1985). A recent reexamination of National Assessment of Educational Progress math and science scores for 1986 shows similar Catholic school advantages for grades 3, 7, and 11 (Lee and Stewart, 1989).

These studies should not lead to the conclusion that Catholic schools have a monopoly on academic excellence. Underlying these averages, there is substantial variation among schools. Clearly, there are some very effective public schools, and some very effective non-Catholic private schools, many of which have been selected for national recognition, as have significant numbers of Catholic elementary and secondary schools. Nor does the research suggest that each Catholic school has reached a level of excellence that precludes any need for improvement. Nevertheless, every comparative study confirms the fact that, on average, Catholic schools are more successful in promoting academic achievement than public and non-Catholic private schools.

There are some educational researchers who take exception to the findings of Catholic school superiority, either by suggesting that alternative analytical procedures should have been used, or by indicating that documented differences in achievement, although "statistically significant" are too small to be of any practical significance (Alexander, 1987; Haertel, 1987; Haertel, James and Levin, 1987b; Walberg and Shanahan, 1983). To each of these arguments there are counter-arguments (e.g., Hoffer, Greeley, and Coleman, 1987). But when the dust settles, it remains clear that Catholic schools, on the average, produce stronger academic outcomes than other school sectors. Their well-documented and unmatched success with students from what Coleman describes as "deficient families" strongly rebuts the claim that positive academic outcomes are predetermined by highly selective admissions policies. The question is not whether Catholic schools succeed, but why they are successful, in spite of limited material resources.

Explanations for Academic Effectiveness

Given that Catholic high school students tend to perform better academically than their public high school counterparts, what are the reasons for these differences? A number of explanations have been offered by various researchers. From our reading of the literature and our own work with Catholic high schools, we have identified six factors that we believe are especially significant in explaining the academic success of these schools. These six concern important public high school/Catholic high school differences in (a) school climate, (b) parental involvement, (c) teacher commitment, (d) leadership and autonomy, (e) the functional community, and (f) the academic curriculum.

School Climate

Schools that encourage academic achievement focus on the importance of scholastic success and on maintaining order and discipline . . . [In such schools] teacher morale is high, and turnover is low. When there are openings, principals recruit and select teachers who share the school's goals and standards. (*What Works*, 1986, p.46)

As exemplified in figure 2, studies comparing Catholic high schools and public high schools on climate factors among teachers and principals almost invariably demonstrate better climate in Catholic high school settings. Ratings of such climate factors show a high degree of correspondence among principals, teachers, and students, lending validity to the measures used. And such public high school/Catholic high school differences are independent of the ethnic/racial or economic composition of the schools (cf. Benson et al., 1986). So while the assessment of school climate is complex, the comparative measures of climate that are available seem to document a distinct Catholic school advantage.

FIGURE 2: School climate in public and Catholic high schools: 1984

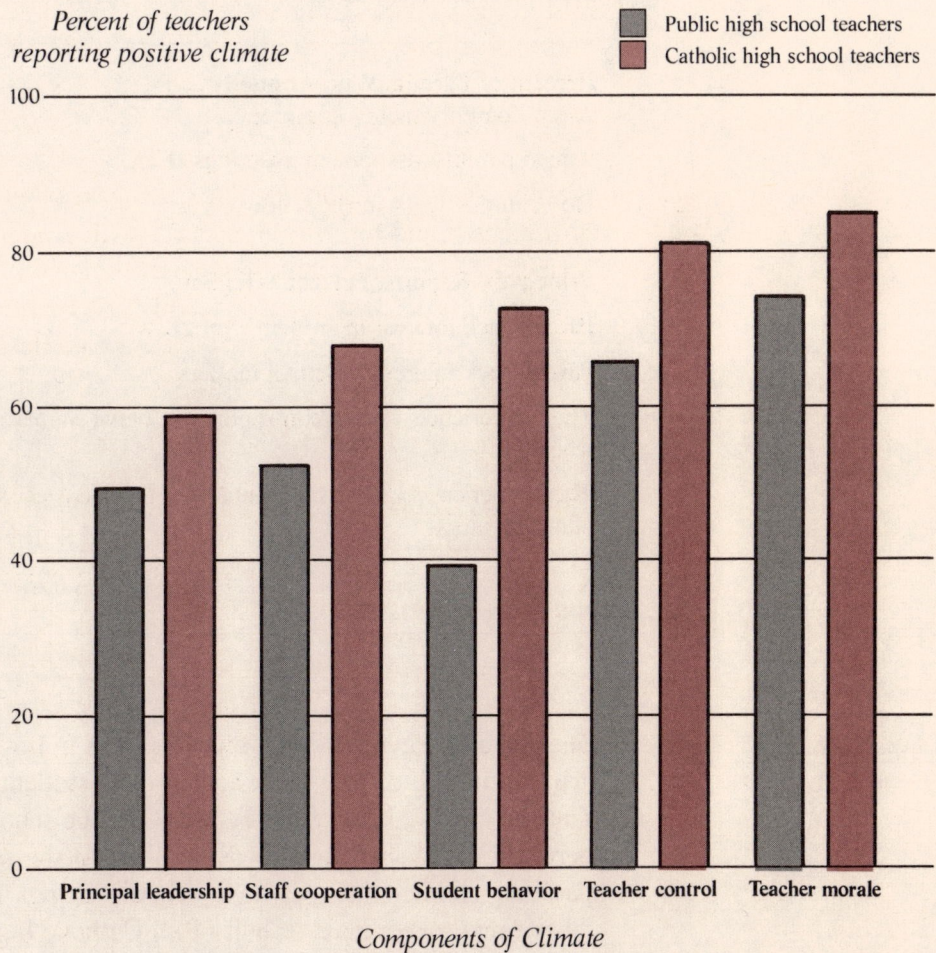

Percent of teachers reporting positive climate

Public high school teachers
Catholic high school teachers

Components of Climate

SOURCE: High School and Beyond Administrator and Teacher Survey. Reproduced from U. S. Department of Education, Center for Education Statistics, *The Condition of Education 1986*, 83.

**Parental
Involvement**

Parental involvement helps children learn more effectively. Teachers who are successful at involving parents in their children's school-work are successful because they work at it. (*What Works*, p. 19)

Data from the *High School and Beyond* study clearly show that parental involvement is more extensive in Catholic high schools. If we believe that increased parental involvement contributes to increased school effectiveness, the evidence suggests that Catholic high schools draw significantly greater strength from their parent communities than their public high school counterparts.

TABLE 1: Indices of Parent Participation in Public High Schools (PHS) and Catholic High Schools (CHS)

	PHS	CHS
Percent of Parents Who Annually . . .		
Attend parent-teacher conferences	39%	56%
Attend parents' association meetings (PTA)	20%	35%
Do volunteer work in the school	27%	46%
Principals' Reports, Percent Who Say. . .		
Parents lack interest in student's progress	53%	7%
Parents lack interest in school matters	55%	18%
They experience verbal confrontations between parents and teachers	22%	8%
They experience verbal confrontations between teachers and administrators	32%	6%

Source: Coleman, J. and Hoffer, T. (1987). *Public and Private High Schools: The Impact of Communities.* New York: Basic Books, pp. 53, 54.

**Teacher
Commitment**

There is ample evidence that most teachers in both public and private schools are committed to their work and to their students. But there are indications that the commitment of teachers in Catholic schools is strengthened by their perception of a shared religious mission. At the same time, the notably lower pay that characterizes Catholic school settings undoubtedly contributes to fairly rapid turnover; over half of all Catholic high school teachers have five years experience or less, and almost a third have two years experience or less. One might expect this to have a negative impact on school climate (see *School Climate*, above). On the contrary, even Catholic high school teachers in schools with limited financial resources, namely those schools in which 10% or more of the students come from families below the federal poverty level, claim high job satisfaction (85% satisfied; Benson et al., 1986).

This seemingly paradoxical circumstance is explained by the Catholic high school teachers' descriptions of their motivations for teaching. They report (Benson et al., 1986) that their three principal reasons for choosing to teach in a Catholic school are a desire to teach in a quality educational environment, the love of teaching, and the understanding that teaching is a kind of ministry. Salary and benefits rank at the bottom of their hierarchy of values. So while they may view teaching in a Catholic high school setting as a temporary state in life, they bring considerable dedication to it while they are there. We submit that teacher commitment in Catholic schools has a powerful and positive impact on student achievement.

Leadership and Autonomy

In an impressive study from the Brookings Institute called *Politics, Markets, and the Organization of Schools*, Chubb and Moe (1986) report evidence that a key factor in school effectiveness is local, in-school control over educational policy, curriculum and staffing. School autonomy enhances the opportunity for educational innovation, and makes a school more likely to respond to the needs of the community it serves. Such local control is much more common in private schools, Catholic high schools among them, than in public high schools:

> The famed Catholic hierarchy plays, by public sector standards, very little role in setting school policy. . . . On all five dimensions [curriculum, instruction, discipline, hiring and firing], the influence of administrative [central office] superiors is far less in Catholic than public schools. (p. 21)

A number of commentators have pointed to a striking example of the differences in administrative structures and control mechanisms in Chicago, where the Catholic and public school systems are among the largest of their types in the country. Until recently, in the Chicago public school system,

> approximately 3,300 employees assigned to the central and district offices create and perform an intricate array of administrative tasks. . . . This is in striking contrast to the *thirty-six* central office administrators employed by the Chicago Archdiocese, which serves a much larger geographical area. (Walberg, Bakalis, Bast, and Baer, 1988, p.12; original italics)

Public school administrators deal with many more administrative constraints (state and federal regulations, unions, voters, the superintendent's office). Public school principals are administrative subordinates in a very complex decision-making system.

Catholic schools stand in sharp contrast. The head administrator of a Catholic school has, in general, considerably more authority and fewer constraints. This allows a strong principal to articulate a vision for the school that draws the faculty, students, and parents together in a community that resembles an extended family.

Academic Curriculum

There is widespread agreement that Catholic schools place more students in academic or college preparatory tracks than do public schools. What is not agreed upon is whether this is because they have more students qualified to do such work, or because they are willing to demand more of their students and expect them to perform at higher levels (Haertel, James, and Levin, 1987a). To the extent that the latter is the case, it indicates a willingness to employ ''self-fulfilling prophecies'' in a positive way:

> Teachers who set and communicate high expectations to all their students obtain greater academic performance from those students than teachers who set low expectations. (*What Works*, p.32)

The *High School and Beyond* studies also indicate that Catholic high schools assign more homework and have more required courses and a generally more rigorous curriculum.

> Student achievement rises significantly when teachers regularly assign homework and students conscientiously do it. The stronger the emphasis on academic courses, the more advanced the subject matter, and the more rigorous the textbooks, the more high school students learn. Subjects that are learned mainly in school rather than at home, such as science and math, are most influenced by the number and kind of courses taken. (*What Works*, p. 41; 59)

The School and the Functional Community

A functional community is a community of people who share a world-view and seek to pass this world-view on to the next generation (Coleman and Hoffer, 1987). In a functional community, schools are designed to help families socialize their children in this world-view. Catholic schools are part of such a community in a way that public schools are not. Anthony Bryk describes some of the elements that combine to generate community both within and beyond the school itself.

> A number of structural features contribute to the formation of positive normative environments in Catholic schools. A relatively small school size, curricula that encourage academic pursuits for all, and extensive student engagement in volunteer service and retreat programs provide concrete experiences of community for both students and faculty. The policies governing assignment of teachers and students to classrooms convey a message that all students are valued. Consistent enforcement of discipline not only maintains social order, but also provides opportunities to articulate personal and social ideals. The result is a predictable and nurturant environment for both the students and adults who form the school community. (Bryk, 1988, p.274)

After describing the programmatic characteristics that he believes help to explain the ability of the Catholic high school to influence the moral life of its students, Bryk goes on to assess the institutional values from which the school's climate and programs are derived.

> A set of moral ideals provides the organizational linchpin that ties the structural features of Catholic high schools to their normative environments. The good Catholic school is impelled by fundamental beliefs about the dignity and worth of each person and a vision of a just social world. These ideas align with liberal educational philosophy that the full development of each student's mind and spirit is the common inheritance of all humanity. This is coupled with a deep commitment to a shared responsibility for our social world that has been enlivened in the post-Vatican II era. Although the religious heritage of Catholic schools is the source of these moral ideals, both the basic ideals and the educational philosophy that derives from them can be articulated on purely secular grounds. (Bryk, 1988, p. 275)

Public schools are, perhaps necessarily, less likely to be rooted in a larger functional community. In the absence of such a shared cultural vision, students consider school to be less relevant to the rest of life, and they therefore devote less energy to learning. Although Bryk argues that the moral ideals generated by the Catholic school's religious identity could be derived from secular postulates in a government school, there is little evidence to suggest that American public education can sustain a coherent vision that acknowledges "full development of each student's mind and *spirit*" and "a just social world" within the prism and prison of "secular pluralism."

Values, Beliefs, and Behaviors

From the point of view of the educational reform movement and the effective schools research, it would be reasonable to conclude that Catholic high schools are already reformed and effective, at least when compared to the public sector. Many of the recommendations of the reform movement are in place in most Catholic high schools. Beneath the new rhetoric of site-based management, teacher empowerment and parental involvement are realities commonly found in Catholic schools.

But is that the point? Are Catholic schools Catholic because they are better schools? Surely not. Consider the following comment from one of the researchers who has criticized James Coleman's methodology and conclusions concerning Catholic high school/public high school differences:

> Private sector schools are not mobilized simply to foster cognitive skills, although this no doubt is very important to many of them. For some such schools, though, building "character" probably rivals the commitment to cognitive development, and for yet others the overriding concern is to stay true to one's faith. I very much doubt that contrasting orientations toward cognitive development is what most distinguishes private from public schools, yet this is what has preoccupied research to date.
>
> The evaluation of effectiveness should be relevant to what both the schools and their clients are trying to accomplish, and this might well direct attention away from cognitive outcomes. I wouldn't be at all surprised, for example, if school sector turned out to be an important factor in affecting religiosity. Here too, though, we still would want to be mindful of internal variations, for there is no single agenda to which even all private sector schools are committed. (Alexander, 1987, p.63)

Thus this critic notes that effectiveness is more than grades in many private schools, and that is certainly the case in Catholic secondary education. While Alexander's motives in enlarging the agenda for private schools may be mixed, his central point is accurate: "... effectiveness should be relevant to what ... the schools and their clients are trying to accomplish." The primary purpose of this study is to examine some of those "other" outcomes, and to determine whether Catholic schooling makes a difference for an array of values and behaviors that more directly address an education aimed at "the full development of each student's mind and spirit, ... and a vision of a just world." For Catholic schools, this is the heart of the matter.

Previous Research on Non-Academic Outcomes

As we noted in the introduction, research concerning non-academic effects of Catholic high schools has been relatively sparse; most research that sets out to examine to what extent schools are "doing their job" understands that job in terms of academic products, measured largely by test scores and diplomas. There have been several studies, however, that have addressed what we call non-academic outcomes, a label with the initial advantage of broad range and the burden of limited specificity. While an exhaustive review of such research is beyond the scope of this presentation, we offer brief summaries of three studies that we consider to be notable contributions in this area. We trust that an examination of these studies coupled with the report of our own work may help to clarify the content and significance of the schools' impact on what students believe and value, as well as what they know.

Convey

Dr. John Convey analyzed the first wave of the *High School and Beyond* data discussed in the previous chapter, but he examined the relatively small number of *value*-related items in the survey, rather than academic outcomes. Comparing Catholics who attend Catholic high schools to Catholics who attend public high schools, he found a number of important differences. Catholic students in Catholic high schools were more likely to attend religious services and rated themselves slightly more religious than their public high school counterparts. He also found that Catholic high school students "had higher family orientation scores, valued children and friendships more, and were less interested in money" than public high school Catholics (p. 48). However, he found that Catholic boys in general, and Catholic high school Catholic boys in particular, were less likely to state that "working to correct social and economic inequalities" was important to them.

As Convey notes, his analysis did not control for a wide variety of background differences that may also have contributed to differences between these two groups of students. However, he suggests that the existence of a shared system of values in the Catholic high school setting probably contributes substantially to reported differences in student responses.

Greeley

Fr. Andrew M. Greeley and his colleagues (e.g., Fee, Greeley, McCready, and Sullivan, 1981; Greeley, McCready, and McCourt, 1976; Greeley and Rossi, 1966) have done important research on the impact of Catholic schooling on later lifestyles and values. Their work differs from other research discussed here in that it is largely retrospective. Rather than studying individuals who are currently in Catholic high schools, their primary approach has been to use survey data from adults who report that they attended Catholic schools in their youth.

A typical example of this research was reported in the volume entitled *Young Catholics in the United States and Canada* (Fee et al., 1981). Employing survey research based on responses from 18- to 30-year-old adults, the study found major differences in various measures of religiousness between those who had received "more than eight years" of Catholic schooling (which would usually mean at least some attendance at Catholic high schools) and those who received "eight years or less." These effects remained even after statistical controls extracted the effects of the religiousness of spouse and family. They summarized their findings as follows:

> 1. Catholic schools are especially important for young people at the religious turning point at the end of the third decade of their lives.
> 2. The schools exercise their effectiveness primarily through an integrating effect: tying people into the Catholic community and Catholic institutions. (p. 126)

This finding anticipates and supports Coleman's later hypothesis about the power of the Catholic school to draw strength from and to contribute to a larger functional community based on shared religious values.

National Catholic Educational Association

The National Catholic Educational Association, with funding from the Ford Foundation, completed a major study of the characteristics and outcomes of Catholic high schools, published in two volumes in 1985 and 1986. The portion of the study which is of particular significance in this context is the second of two volumes, *Catholic High Schools: Their Impact on Low-Income Students* (Benson, Yeager, Wood, Guerra, and Manno, 1986). The report was based on extensive surveys of 1,000 teachers and 8,000 students in 106 Catholic high schools in the United States, and in-depth field studies of a subset of five schools. All these schools were chosen because ten percent or more of their students came from families whose incomes were below the federal poverty line.

Unlike other studies described in this report, this study included only Catholic high school students. Its findings can only be descriptive, and therefore cannot provide the comparative data needed to support exclusive attribution of student beliefs and attitudes to their experiences of Catholic high schools. Nonetheless, its findings are worth noting. In mild contrast to Convey's finding of somewhat limited student interest in social issues, "establishing oneself as a contributing member of society" was ranked high as a life goal for all students in these low-income serving schools regardless of the students' family income; self-centered goals were ranked low. Freshman reported having engaged in more anti-social behavior as eighth graders than they did as freshman, suggesting that students perceived that the Catholic high school environment had an inhibiting effect on such behaviors. Furthermore, students' religiousness was found to have a modest but statistically significant inhibiting effect on anti-social behaviors, prejudice, and sexism. And, in an interesting analysis of correlations, school climate factors (e.g., community, morale, nurturance) predicted value and religion outcomes better than course work. In short, this study offers additional support for the conviction that student values are strongly influenced by the experience of school as community.

Summary

Each of the previous studies provides valuable insights into understanding the effects of Catholic high school training on various value and behavior outcomes. Taken together, these studies offer generally positive evidence about the capacity of the Catholic high school to influence the beliefs, values and behaviors of its students. And yet something is missing. What is needed is a study which, like Convey's, compares Catholic high school and public high school students on values measures and is based on a major national data set, but which also, like the Greeley and NCEA studies, incorporates analytical controls for some of the important background differences between the two groups. The remainder of this monograph is devoted to describing precisely such a study.

The Present Study

Where the Data Come From

The present study uses data gathered as part of an on-going survey of all high school seniors in the United States entitled *Monitoring the Future*. Detailed information concerning the survey's methodology can be obtained from any one of its annual data books (e.g., Johnston, Bachman, and O'Malley, 1986). Each spring, a nationally representative sample of approximately 16,000 high school seniors from 125 high schools complete questionnaires ranging in length from approximately 300 to 800 items each. The questionnaires consist of a core of approximately 90 common items, incorporated into five forms, each one of which is administered to one-fifth of the sample. The various versions of the questionnaire cover a wide variety of topics. In view of the fact that the National Institute on Drug Abuse provides major funding for the *Monitoring the Future* project, more than 40% of the questions deal with drug abuse, but the survey also addresses a wide variety of other content areas: attitudes toward education, work and leisure; gender roles and the family; religion; social problems; race relations; delinquency; and various personality characteristics. The results of these surveys are made available in two forms; the annual data books mentioned earlier (Johnston et al., 1986) and the data tapes making the individual-level data available for analyses. In order to conduct our analyses of Catholic school effects, we commissioned the Survey Research Center of the Institute for Social Research at the University of Michigan, which conducts the annual survey, to prepare a special set of data tapes. At our request, the Center coded (for the first time) whether each senior in the survey attended a high school that was public (approximately 100 such schools per year), Catholic (15-20 schools each year), or "other private" (2-3 schools yearly) for the data from 1976 to 1985.

Methodology

The Data Set

The *Monitoring the Future* data set is huge by any reasonable standards, with 16,000 respondents in each of 10 years answering more than 300 questions. Some method of nominating a subset of the data to be examined was required. Since the "other private" high school sample was too small for separate analysis it was dropped from the data set (a procedure also followed by most of the researchers who conducted the first *High School and Beyond* analyses). Second, the urban-rural distribution of the schools in the sample led to the decision to restrict our analyses to schools located in urban areas and their adjoining counties.

A third decision was to restrict our analyses solely to Catholics. While this decreases the public high school sample by two-thirds, the overall effects of this decision on the analyses are beneficial. Such a "Catholic-to-Catholic" comparison controls for an entire set of otherwise imponderable cultural, ethnic, and philosophical characteristics bound up in the word "Catholic" (cf. Occhiogrosso, 1987).

Lastly, due to the relatively small number of minority students in the samples, no separate analyses by race or ethnic group were performed.

This distillation of the data set led to some relatively small samples (e.g., 200) in individual years for the analyses of items derived from only one of the five forms of the survey. In order to retain the opportunity to examine important values issues contained in one form but not in the core, all analyses reported here used one or more of three combined data sets: 1976-1978; 1979-1982; 1983-1985.

Background and Outcome Variables

The final selection of analytical variables from the vast collection presented by the *Monitoring the Future* data set was based on two criteria: (a) retaining as many of the background variables in the core as possible in order to strengthen the analytical capability to uniquely identify school effects, and (b) choosing areas that seemed most relevant to the stated mission of Catholic secondary education. The resulting set of variables was large, and an extended discussion of the exact items in the scales and their reliabilities is beyond the scope of this report. A separate technical report presents psychometric data and detailed statistical summary tables underpinning the analyses reported here.[1]

The variables given attention in this analysis can be divided into two categories: *background* variables and *outcome* variables. The background variables used are summarized in Table 2. The variable names shown in Table 2 are used throughout the remainder of this report to describe differences between groups of students and linkages between sets of background variables and outcomes. The range, content, and number of items used to measure these 31 outcome variables, in six domains, are presented in Table 3.

TABLE 2: Family and Personal Background Variables

VARIABLE	NUMBER OF ITEMS	SCALE OR ITEM CONTENT
Gender	1	Whether the respondent is male ($=1$) or female ($=2$)
SRegion NERegion WRegion	1	Whether the student is in the Southern, Northeastern, or Western region of the United States (as defined by the US Bureau of the Census; North Central [Midwest] is a noncoded comparison group)
Urban	1	The size of the community in which the respondent grew up: farm or country ($=1$); small city or town under 50,000 ($=2$); city 50-100,000 ($=3$); large city (100-500,000) or its suburb ($=4$); very large city (over 500,000) or its suburb ($=5$)
Father Mother	1 1	Whether the student's father (mother) or (fe)male guardian is present in the household
Parents' Education	2	The mean of the father and mother's educational level as reported by the student: grade school ($=1$); some high school ($=2$); completed high school ($=3$); some college ($=4$); completed college ($=5$); graduate education ($=6$)
Mother Worked	1	Whether the student's mother had "a paid job (half time or more) while the student was growing up": NO ($=1$); some of the time ($=2$); most of the time ($=3$); all or nearly all the time ($=4$)
Hours Worked	1	The number of hours per school week the student has a paid job: 0 ($=1$); 5 or less ($=2$); 6-10 ($=3$); 11-15 ($=4$); 16-20 ($=5$); 21-25 ($=6$); 26-30 ($=7$); more than 30 ($=8$)
Nights Out	1	The number of nights during a typical school week that the student goes out for "fun and recreation;" less than one ($=1$); one ($=2$); two ($=3$); three ($=4$); 4-5 ($=5$); 6-7 ($=6$)

TABLE 3: Outcome Variables

CONCEPT LABEL	# ITEMS	SCALE CONTENT
Social Values		
Militarism	5	Willingness to go war; important that US be a "military power"
Pro-Marriage	3	Reject "monogamy too restrictive" "couples should cohabit before marriage"
Racial Acceptance	4	Accept close social relations with persons of other races
Equal Opportunity	4	Endorsement of equal pay and career opportunities for men and women
Materialism	2	Important to have latest fashions and "keep up with the Joneses"
Educational Values		
Pro-School	4	Positive attitude toward school and school work perceived relevant
College Plans	1	Intention to attend college
Cutting School	1	Number of school days "skipped", last 4 weeks
Concern for People		
Community Involvement	1	Frequency of participation in community affairs or volunteer work
Make a Difference	1	Important in life to "make a contribution to society"
Support Social Justice	1	Importance of working to correct social and economic inequality
Helping Profession	1	Important that career offers opportunity to be directly helpful to others
Concern for Others	6	Rejection of attitudes that "we ought to only worry about our own"
Contribute Money	5	Likelihood of contributing to various charities, including church
At-Risk Behaviors		
Delinquency	8	Frequency of violent and illegal behaviors in the last year
Risk-Taking	2	Desire to engage in "risky" or "dangerous" behavior
Cigarette Use	1	Cigarette use, previous month
Alcohol Use	1	Alcohol use, past year
Binge Drinking	1	Number of times had five or more drinks in a row, past two weeks
Marijuana Use	1	Marijuana use, previous year
Cocaine Use	1	Cocaine use, previous year
Illicit Drug Use	1	Ever used any illicit drug (yes/no)
Perception of Self		
Self-Esteem	8	Positive self-image
Internal Control	7	Can influence course of own life
Pessimism	4	World will soon end in disaster
Loneliness	5	Loneliness and social isolation
Happiness	1	Feeling "happy these days"
Faith and Church		
Church Attendance	1	Frequency of attending religious services
Importance of Religion	1	Importance of religion in own life
Influence of Churches	1	Support increase in influence of churches in daily life
Church Contributions	1	Likely to give money to religious groups

Descriptive Statistics

The Current Picture

Table 4 presents means on all of the background and outcome variables for all students by *School Type*. The first analysis examines data from the most recent period, 1983-1985. Trends over time are discussed in the next section. Analyses of the determinants of the outcome measures follow the discussion of trends.

Family and personal background. Catholic seniors in Catholic high schools differ from Catholic seniors in public high schools on every FAMILY AND PERSONAL BACKGROUND variable considered here. Catholic high school seniors report that they grew up in larger *Urban* communities, that their *Parents' Education* was higher, that it is less likely that their *Mother Worked* while they were growing up, and that they have fewer *Hours Worked* and *Nights Out* during the average school week than public high school students. They are also more likely to live in a family with a *Father* present (87% vs 81%). Thus, the proportion of two-parent families is higher for Catholic high school than for public high school Catholic seniors (85% vs 79%)—a more "traditional" portrait for the families of Catholic high school seniors.

Outcome measures. Differences between Catholic high school and public high school student means displayed numerically in Table 4 are portrayed in Table 5 in a way that distinguishes positive (+) from negative (-) value outcomes. Catholic high school seniors have stronger *Pro-Marriage* attitudes, and are less supportive of *Militarism* than their public high school peers. They are more likely to report that they intend to graduate from a four-year college (*College Plans*) and to express CONCERN FOR PEOPLE in a variety of ways, including contributing money. Their reports of AT-RISK BEHAVIORS show that Catholic seniors in Catholic high schools consistently report higher *Alcohol Use*, but are less likely to report ever engaging in *Illicit Drug Use* than Catholic seniors in public high schools. They also display less *Pessimism*. Lastly, Catholic high school seniors report they are more religious on three of the four FAITH AND CHURCH measures: *Church Attendance*, *Importance of Religion*, and *Church Contributions*.

Table 6 examines gender differences. Boys report more *Militarism* than girls, and girls display stronger support for *Materialism*. On each of the remaining SOCIAL VALUES, however, *Pro-Marriage*, *Racial Acceptance*, and *Equal Opportunity*, girls show higher rates of endorsement than boys. There are no gender differences on EDUCATIONAL VALUES or PERSPECTIVE ON SELF. The gender differences on CONCERN FOR PEOPLE and FAITH

TABLE 4: Catholic Seniors, 1983-1985

	TOTAL	PHS	CHS
FAMILY AND PERSONAL BACKGROUND			
% live with mother or female guardian	94	94	96
% live with father or male guardian	83	81	87
Urban (1-5)	3.13	2.95	3.51
Parents' Education (1-6)	3.87	3.76	4.11
Mother Worked (1-4)	2.19	2.25	2.07
Hours Worked (1-8)	4.19	4.29	3.98
Nights Out (1-6)	3.55	3.59	3.44
OUTCOMES			
Social Values			
Militarism (1-5)	3.20	3.27	3.06
Pro-Marriage (1-5)	3.45	3.34	3.70
Racial Acceptance (1-4)	3.12	3.13	3.10
Equal Opportunity (1-5)	4.53	4.52	4.55
Materialism (1-4)	2.51	2.51	2.49
Educational Values			
Pro-School (1-5)	3.30	3.34	3.22
College Plans (1-4)	2.96	2.82	3.28
Cutting School (1-7)	1.60	1.71	1.35
Concern for People			
Community Involvement (1-5)	2.00	1.94	2.13
Make a Difference (1-4)	2.64	2.59	2.75
Support Social Justice (1-4)	2.13	2.12	2.16
Helping Profession (1-4)	3.26	3.24	3.29
Concern for Others (1-5)	3.81	3.75	3.95
Contribute Money (1-6)	3.71	3.65	3.86
At-Risk Behaviors			
Delinquency (1-5)	1.41	1.40	1.44
Risk-Taking (1-5)	3.01	2.99	3.03
Cigarette Use (1-7)	1.76	1.80	1.67
Alcohol Use (1-7)	4.67	4.60	4.83
Binge Drinking (1-6)	2.06	2.03	2.13
Marijuana Use (1-7)	2.46	2.50	2.37
Cocaine Use (1-7)	1.33	1.36	1.26
% ever using an illicit drug	65	66	62
Perceptions of Self			
Self-Esteem (1-5)	4.08	4.07	4.10
Internal Control (1-5)	3.79	3.77	3.81
Pessimism (1-5)	2.75	2.79	2.68
Loneliness (1-5)	2.39	2.40	2.35
Happiness (1-3)	2.07	2.07	2.08
Faith and Church			
Church Attendance (1-4)	3.10	2.94	3.47
Importance of Religion (1-4)	2.85	2.77	3.05
Influence of Churches (1-5)	3.28	3.23	3.39
Church Contributions (1-6)	4.48	4.38	4.73

TABLE 5: Differences Among Catholic Seniors in Catholic High Schools (CHS) and Public High Schools (PHS), 1983-1985

DOMAIN	CHS HIGHER THAN PHS	PHS HIGHER THAN CHS
Social Values	Pro-Marriage (+)	Militarism (−)
Educational Values	College Plans (+)	Cutting School (−)
Concern for People	Community Involvement (+) Contribute Money (+) Concern for Others (+)	
At-Risk Behavior	Alcohol Use (−) Binge Drinking (−)	Cigarette Use (−) Cocaine Use (−) Illicit Drug Use (−)
Perspective on Self		Pessimism (−)
Faith and Church	Church Attendance (+) Importance of Religion (+) Church Contributions (+)	

AND CHURCH nearly completely parallel the *School Type* differences, with girls showing the more "Catholic" pattern—not surprising in light of the consistent finding that girls, overall, are more religious than boys (e.g., Argyle and Beit-Hallahmi, 1975). Lastly, boys display higher incidences of all AT-RISK BEHAVIORS than girls, except for *Cigarette Use*, which girls engage in more frequently.

Summary. In general, girls, and to a lesser extent, Catholic seniors in Catholic high schools, report more positive values and behaviors than their counterparts. These findings, we stress again, are *descriptive* differences occurring among student subgroups. From the data presented here, it would be premature to make any claims about the effect of Catholic schooling. The examination of school effects will be addressed later in this chapter, in the discussion of determinants of outcomes.

Ten-Year Trends

Are seniors recently graduating from Catholic high schools more or less likely than their predecessors to report beliefs, values and behaviors consonant with the purposes of Catholic schools? In order to examine trends in the attitude and behaviors of Catholic high school seniors, we compared and contrasted

TABLE 6: Gender Differences Among Catholic Seniors, 1983-1985
(Public and Catholic Schools Combined)

DOMAIN	GIRLS HIGHER THAN BOYS	BOYS HIGHER THAN GIRLS
Social Values	Pro-Marriage (+) Racial Acceptance (+) Equal Opportunity (+) Materialism (−)	Militarism (−)
Concern for People	Helping Profession (+) Concern for Others (+) Contribute Money (+)	
At-Risk Behavior	Cigarette Use (−)	Delinquency (−) Risk-Taking (−) Alcohol Use (−) Binge Drinking (−) Marijuana (−) Cocaine Use (−) Illicit Drug Use (−)
Faith and Church	Church Attendance (+) Importance of Religion (+) Church Contributions (+)	

data from three time periods: 1976-1978, 1979-1982, and 1983-1985. Table 7 provides a summary of 10-year trends for Catholic seniors in public and Catholic high schools, organized graphically to illustrate nine possible variations in changes over time. In those instances in which appropriate statistical analyses indicate that particular trends differ as a function of *Gender* or *School Type*, that is noted in the text.

Family and Personal Background. FAMILY AND PERSONAL BACKGROUND variables are italicized wherever they occur in Table 7. While the percent of the seniors who report that they are living with either parent and the size of their home towns showed no net change, each of the other FAMILY AND PERSONAL BACKGROUND variables have shown changes. The students' reports of their *Parents' Education* increased between Period 1 and Period 2, but then leveled off.

The number of students reporting that their *Mother Worked* has increased in recent years, but more markedly for public high school students. Students

TABLE 7: Ten Year Trends in *Background* and Outcome Measures for Catholic Seniors, 1976-1985

10 YEAR TREND	DESCRIPTION OF TREND	MEASURES DISPLAYING TREND	
A	No change over 10 years	• *Mother* • *Father* • *Hours Worked* • Pro-School • Support Social Justice • Helping Profession • Concern for Others • Contribute Money	• Delinquency • Happiness • Community Involvement • Racial Acceptance • Make a Difference • Church Attendance • Influence of Churches • Church Contributions
B	Decrease in 1979-1982, Increase 1983 - 1985	• Materialism	
C	Increase in 1979-1982, Decrease 1983 - 1985	• *Urban* • Binge Drinking • Illicit Drug Use • Alcohol use • Pessimism	
D	Increase across 10 years	• Equal Opportunity	
E	Increase in 1983 - 1985	• *Mother Worked* • Risk-Taking	
F	Increase in 1979 - 1982	• *Parents Education* • Cocaine Use • Importance of Religion • College Plans	• Pro-Marriage • Self-Esteem • Internal Control
G	Decrease over 10 years	• Cutting School	
H	Decrease in 1983 - 1985	• Militarism • Marijuana Use	
I	Decrease in 1979 - 1982	• *Nights Out* • Cigarette Use • Loneliness	

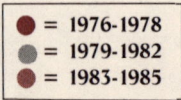

● = 1976-1978
● = 1979-1982
● = 1983-1985

show some curious differences by subgroup concerning their own *Hours Worked*. Although the combined group shows no change over 10 years, public high school students as a group, and girls as a group, report an "inverted-U" pattern over time, while Catholic high school students as a group, and boys as a group, report "decline and then plateau" data. Lastly, *Nights Out* declined for everybody between Period 1 and Period 2, and have been relatively constant since then.

Social Values. None of the concepts in this area showed the complex differences in subgroups discussed for the background variables, and one, *Racial Acceptance*, has shown no change at all over the period (it has remained at a level of 3.1 on a 4-point scale). Among the other variables, *Militarism*, constant between Period 1 and Period 2, showed a marked decline between Periods 2 and 3. *Pro-Marriage* attitudes increased slightly between Periods 1 and 2 and have since been constant. Acceptance of *Equal Opportunity* for men and women showed an increase between Periods 2 and 3, and now stands at a mean level of 4.55 on a 5-point scale, perhaps a practical upper limit, and the highest percentage agreement of any concept examined here. Lastly, *Materialism*, which had declined among Catholic seniors between 1976-78 and 1979-82, has experienced a resurgence to its former levels. Thus the reports of increasing materialism among students would be more accurately described as a return to levels of materialism reported by students five to seven year earlier.

Educational Values. *Pro-School* attitudes have remained essentially unchanged. *Cutting School* has been declining in public high schools, but rose in Catholic high schools between Period 1 and 2, falling back to its previous levels between Periods 2 and 3. However, the rate of *Cutting School* in Catholic high schools remained well below that in public high schools during the entire period, showing the same magnitude of difference as displayed in Table 4. *College Plans* have displayed an increasing and then a fairly steady profile, with the increase somewhat stronger in Catholic high schools than in public high schools. As a group, however, boys' intention to attend a four-year college rose from Period 1 (2.77) to Period 2 (3.08) and then fell somewhat after that (2.95); girls have shown steady increase from Period 1 (2.55) to Period 3 (2.98), eventually "catching up" with boys.

Concern for People. None of these variables showed any change over the three time periods examined here, either overall, or for any of the subgroups analyzed.

At-Risk Behaviors. The measure of *Delinquency* (involving such behaviors as fighting, theft, vandalism, and trouble with the police), showed no change over the ten years examined here. The propensity for *Risk-Taking*, however, did increase significantly from 1979-1972 to 1983-1985. Each of the remaining AT-RISK BEHAVIORS, all of them dealing with drug use, has changed during the period, some for the better, some for the worse.

Cigarette Use declined between Period 1 and 2, and has leveled off since then. Both *Alcohol Use* and the related concept of *Binge Drinking* showed the inverted-U rise-and-fall pattern over these ten years. *Marijuana Use* has also shown consistent decline over the same period, and the percent of seniors that reported some experience with *Illicit Drug Use* rose to 70%, and then fell back to its original level (65%) over the three periods.

The one drug that has shown a net increase over this time period is *Cocaine*. This index is one of use in the previous year, and the scale ranges from 1 to 7, 1 being "never" and 2 being 1-2 times in the last year. The highest mean for any group (boys in public high schools during Period 3) is 1.42, so that even at its highest, its use could not be considered rampant, but both boys and girls, in both public high schools and Catholic high schools, show a net increase between Periods 1 and 3.

Perceptions of Self. *Self-Esteem* and *Internal Control* show very similar profiles over the three periods considered here; both rise between periods 1 and 2, and then level off. *Loneliness* shows the opposite pattern, declining initially, and then leveling off. *Pessimism* shows the inverted-U pattern, rising for Period 2, but then returning to approximately its earlier level. *Happiness* remained very constant, at almost precisely 2 ("pretty happy") on a three-point scale. (The range of scores for all groups and periods was 2.00 to 2.10.)

Faith and Church. Neither *Church Attendance* nor the likelihood that the students would make *Church Contributions* changed over this time period. *Importance of Religion* has shown an increase in the most recent period over the previous seven years in Catholic high schools, but has risen and then fallen in public high schools, a variation masked by the plateau from 1982 to 1985, describing the net effect in table 7.

Summary. Twelve of the 31 outcomes examined in this report show no significant changes across ten years. Prominent among that group is the entire list of items and scales addressing CONCERN FOR PEOPLE. Note also that *Materialism* shows no net change, although in recent years it has been rising to previous levels. In addition, four outcomes, all negative, are declining to previous levels: *Alcohol Use, Binge Drinking, Illicit Drug Use,* and *Pessimism.*

Two outcomes have shown an overall increase among Catholics in both Catholic high schools and public high schools in this period, while five have decreased. Only two of these seven changes would be considered negative: the Period 1-2 increase in *Cocaine Use* in the previous year, and the increase in the attitude in favor of *Risk-Taking*. The other five changes represent positive or desirable trends: decreases in *Cutting School, Militarism, Marijuana Use, Cigarette Use*, and *Loneliness*.

There are many possible reasons for these relatively positive trends between 1976 and 1985. In the next section, our analysis suggests that *Nights Out*, a FAMILY AND PERSONAL BACKGROUND variable that declined in this same 10-year period for all Catholic seniors, is a major predictor of three of these five positive outcomes. Other research has consistently confirmed that *Importance of Religion*, at least in Catholic high schools, during this same 10-year period may account for some of the other positive changes in outcome variables.

Determinants of Outcomes: What "Causes" the Differences?

Methodology

The final set of analyses employed a statistical technique called "multiple regression." The purpose of this procedure is to determine the extent to which *each* of several possible predictor variables, or "causes," influences another variable. For example, is the degree of *Militarism* expressed by a given student more a reflection of the school they attend, their gender, or their parents' education?

In doing these analyses, the effects of all of the 12 FAMILY AND PERSONAL BACKGROUND variables discussed above, plus *Importance of Religion* and *School Type* were examined for their influence on each of the outcome variables shown in Table 3. Across these 31 analyses, 4 of the 14 predictor variables had frequent and significant influence on the outcome variables: *Gender, Nights Out, Importance of Religion*, and *School Type*. We will discuss the effect of each of these four variables on a number of important outcomes; the analysis is summarized in table 8.

Social Values

Gender is the single strongest variable associated with *Racial Acceptance, Equal Pay*, and the rejection of *Militarism*. SOCIAL VALUES are also shaped to a degree by school effects. Catholic high school seniors are more likely than

TABLE 8: Relative Strength of Variables in Predicting Outcome Variables

	BEING FEMALE	IMPORTANCE OF RELIGION	NIGHTS OUT	ATTEND CATHOLIC HIGH SCHOOL
SOCIAL VALUES				
Militarism	▼▼▼▼			▼
Pro-Marriage		▲▲▲		▲
Racial Acceptance	▲▲			
Equal Opportunity	▲▲▲▲▲▲▲			
EDUCATIONAL VALUES				
Pro-School		▲▲▲	▼▼	▼
College Plans			▼	▲
Cutting School			▲▲▲	▼▼
CONCERN FOR PEOPLE				
Community Involvement		▲▲▲▲		
Make a Difference		▲▲▲		▲
Helping Profession	▲▲▲▲▲	▲		
Concern for Others	▲▲▲	▲▲▲	▼	▲
Contribute Money	▲▲	▲▲▲▲		▲
AT-RISK BEHAVIORS				
Delinquency	▼▼▼▼		▲▲	
Risk-Taking	▼▼▼▼		▲	
Cigarette Use	▲		▲▲▲	
Alcohol Use			▲▲▲▲	
Binge Drinking	▼		▲▲▲▲	
Marijuana Use		▼	▲▲▲▲▲	
Cocaine Use			▲▲▲▲	
Illicit Drug Use		▼	▲▲▲▲	
FAITH & CHURCH				
Church Attendance		▲▲▲▲▲		▲
Importance of Religion	▲			▲▲▲
Influence of Churches		▲▲▲▲▲▲▲		
Church Contributions		▲▲▲▲▲▲		

Note: In this table, ▲ signs indicate that the attribute at the top of the column is associated with an increase in the outcome, and ▼ signs indicate that it is associated with a decrease in the outcome. Numbers of ▲ and ▼ signs are comparable ONLY WITHIN a given outcome variable, and not between outcome variables.

their public high school counterparts to reject *Militarism*. This theme has received emphasis in the recent pastoral letter of the bishops of the United States entitled *The Challenge of Peace: God's Promise and Our Response* (National Conference of Catholic Bishops, 1983). It would seem that the concern for peace has apparently been incorporated within the curriculum of Catholic high schools with some degree of success, inasmuch as Catholic seniors in Catholic high schools show greater concern about this issue than Catholic seniors in public high schools. Similarly, there is a stronger *Pro-Marriage* attitude displayed by students attending Catholic schools.

Educational Values

The *School Type* distinction is a prime factor in explaining differences in students' EDUCATIONAL VALUES. *School Type* has a significant effect on each of three educational values: Catholic high school seniors are less likely to report *Cutting School*, more likely to have *College Plans*, and *less* likely to express *Pro-School* attitudes. The third finding is all the more interesting and anomolous in light of the strong positive association between *Importance of Religion* and *Pro-School*. Thus, despite the fact that Catholic high school seniors rate religion as more important than public high school seniors, and religiousness is generally positively correlated with liking school, Catholic high school seniors are more negative toward school. Some speculations about this anomolous finding are provided in chapter 4.

Not surprisingly, those who report more *Nights Out* were less likely to be *Pro-School*, somewhat less likely to have *College Plans*, and notably *more* likely to report that they had been *Cutting School.*

Concern for People

A strong relationship between each of these measures of *Concern for People* and *Importance of Religion* was quite notable. The student's self-reported religiousness was the single strongest predictor of *Community Involvement*, and was also strongly related to whether the student donated money to various charities. *Gender* was also strongly related to each of these measures, except for *Community Involvement*; other than community involvement, girls scored higher in each of the areas within this domain.

School Type showed small but significant impacts on three measures: *Concern for Others*, *Contribute Money*, and *Make a Difference*. The finding concerning *Contribute Money* must be viewed with caution, since it included an item concerning contributing money to churches and religious organizations, and the more religious Catholic high school seniors are more likely to say they will do that (see below, under FAITH AND CHURCH.) Nonetheless, these two findings reflect a rejection of selfishness, and a desire to be actively involved in bringing about positive societal change.

One concept in this area, *Support for Social Justice*, was not explained by this particular group of predictors. However, it is a single-item measure and did not show school or gender differences in our earlier discussions.

At-Risk Behaviors

Of eight categories of deviant or norm-breaking behavior, *Nights Out* is the single strongest contributor by far for all of the listed behaviors and attitudes except *Delinquency* and *Risk-Taking*. In those two cases, *Nights Out* was important, but *Gender* (being male) was stronger. *Importance of Religion* is negatively related to both *Marijuana Use* in the previous 12 months, and whether the student has ever engaged in *Illicit Drug Use*.

It is notable that none of the many school differences in at-risk behavior reported in the descriptive analyses of the data set appear in this analyses. The most likely explanation is that, given the school differences reflected in *Nights out*, it is not school differences *per se*, but differences in the number of *Nights Out* that has primary impact on these AT-RISK BEHAVIORS. Some possible explanations for the effects of *Nights Out* and the relationship of those effects to *School Type* are presented in chapter 4.

Perceptions of Self

PERCEPTIONS OF SELF, which includes the personality variables of *Self-Esteem, Internal Control, Pessimism, Loneliness*, and *Happiness*, were not significantly predicted by any of the fourteen background variables used in these analyses. A reasonable explanation for this finding is that each of these five variables is unusually volatile for adolescents. Each might be expected to fluctuate over broad ranges depending on how the individual student's life is going at the moment. Given that students' self-concepts are more strongly influenced by transitory external events, it is not surprising that broad personality constructs do not predict these variables for high school seniors.

Faith and Church

Not surprisingly, *Church Attendance*, the desire to see the *Influence of Churches* increase in society, and the intention to make *Church Contributions* are all primarily functions of *Importance of Religion*. But what non-religious factors predict *Importance of Religion*? Both *School Type* (Catholic high school) and *Gender* (female) are strongly related. There is also a school effect for *Church Attendance*, and because the item that measures it asks about average weekly attendance, it is unlikely to be attributable to occasional Mass attendance during special liturgical functions held in Catholic high schools.

Summary

Among a range of correlations strong and weak we would underscore several particularly significant relationships. The strong impact of *Nights Out* on AT-RISK BEHAVIORS is one; its negative impact on EDUCATIONAL VALUES is another. *Gender* shows strong effect here, associated with CONCERN FOR

PEOPLE and AT-RISK BEHAVIORS. *Importance of Religion* displays a strong positive influence on CONCERN FOR PEOPLE, and a strong negative influence on some forms of drug use. Some of the differences that formerly appeared to be a function of *School Type* here appear instead to be differences in the number of *Nights Out* spent by the two groups, and perhaps in their religiousness. At the same time, we see repeated and independent school effects in these analyses. Social, educational, and religious values all show influences of schooling, not reducible to any of the other individual differences measured here.

CHAPTER 4

Summary and Conclusions

Initial Thoughts

In the course of this research we have considered three different perspectives on Catholic students in public and Catholic high schools, namely differences between groups, 10-year trends and determinants of outcomes, an area within which we are particularly interested in measuring the unique impact of the school on student beliefs and values. Here is a summary of our key findings and our initial judgments about what these findings mean.

Differences Between Groups

The patterns of group differences observed in Table 4 are of some interest. Some of these differences disappeared when examined in more sophisticated regression analyses. However, the overall pattern was basically robust and persistent. Catholic high school affiliation influences some SOCIAL VALUES, all EDUCATIONAL VALUES, and two of the four FAITH AND CHURCH constructs. In terms of mature values and behaviors, girls look better than boys, except for the continuation of recent trends concerning their smoking habits.

Ten-Year Trends

Concerning trends over the ten-year period described by these data, one might say that "the market is broadly higher in moderate trading." Among the background measures, it is not surprising to see that both *Parent's Education* and whether or not *Mother Worked* have increased in recent years, and *Nights Out* have decreased; all the other family background characteristics have shown no net change.

On the "outcomes market," 13 are unchanged while five show no net change, displaying a curvilinear pattern that ends where it began. Five undesirable outcomes have shown net decline while six desirable outcomes have increased. Only two undesirable outcomes, *Cocaine Use*, and *Risk-Taking*, a corollary of drug use, have increased. The increase in *Cocaine Use* over the past ten years has been minimal, however; from 1.15 to 1.33 where "1" means "never," and "2" means 1-2 time in the past year. Likewise, the increase in propensity for *Risk-Taking* has been from 2.81 to 3.01 on a five-point scale on which 3.00 means "Neither disagree nor agree."

In general, then, the pattern of these indicators is positive. While there were some differences in these patterns as a function of *School Type*, except in the case of the complex patterns for *Importance of Religion* noted earlier, the differences tended to be relatively minor, and did not affect the overall differences between the two types of schools.

Determinants of Outcomes

Analyses revealed that, in addition to the large impact of *Gender, School Type* also had independent influence on SOCIAL VALUES, and *Importance of Religion* was a major factor in CONCERN FOR PEOPLE. Femaleness and *Importance of Religion* inhibited AT-RISK BEHAVIORS (except for *Cigarette Use* which was higher for girls), while *Nights Out* tended to be strongly positively correlated with AT-RISK BEHAVIORS. *School Type* was also a major predictor of EDUCATIONAL VALUES, but the set of FAMILY AND PERSONAL BACKGROUND variables employed in these analyses did not predict PERCEPTIONS OF SELF.

School Effects

A major purpose of this study has been to examine the relative impact of public and Catholic high school attendance on the values and behaviors of Catholic seniors. While we have discussed the relationship of school type to a number of findings, we turn now to a comprehensive analysis of school effects. This discussion is based on the findings of the regression analyses, and our interpretation of those results.

Social Values

The findings regarding school effects in this area are notable. *School Type* is the only variable aside from *Gender* to show an effect on *Militarism*, and, as we have noted, this finding offers some evidence of the Catholic high school's response to the growing concern within the Catholic community for education that promotes peace and justice. While *Pro-Marriage*, not surprisingly, is strongly influenced by the rated *Importance of Religion*, there is also an independent school effect. Since *Pro-Marriage* can reasonably be treated as a proxy variable for sexual ethics (given that the survey items deal with monogamy and non-marital cohabitation), this indicates a positive impact of Catholic schooling over and above Catholic cultural background and commitment to Catholic ideology. The absence of a statistically significant school effect on *Racial Acceptance* may be due in part to ceiling effects, since the mean of this variable is higher (as a percent of its total range) than any other scale except for *Equal Opportunity* and *Self-Esteem*. There may be little room for improvement, at least insofar as this scale measures racial acceptance.

Educational Values

It is here that *School Type* has its most consistent effects, and its most paradoxical. Attending a Catholic high school is negatively associated with *Cutting School*, perhaps because of generally tighter discipline in Catholic high schools. It is positively associated with *College Plans*, independent of *Parental Education*. This is a particularly impressive effect, since higher parental education is associated with greater familiarity with the benefits of higher education, with higher family income, and with greater likelihood of being financially able to attend college. The association of Catholic high schools with educational aspirations that transcend these family influences is impressive evidence of the uniquely supportive and powerful educational climate in Catholic schools. But then the enigma. The *Pro-School* measure, consisting of an index of items measuring liking for school, interest in school, and the perceived relevance of school work, is lower in Catholic high schools than public high schools, even in spite of the fact that, in general, religious students are more *Pro-School* than non-religious students. Why should that be the case? Previous research, such as the *High School and Beyond* studies (e.g., Coleman et al., 1982), have shown that Catholic high schools have greater academic rigor, more homework, and more discipline; they provide serious learning environments. It is not hard to believe that this level of discipline is not universally well-received by adolescents. It is similarly not hard to believe that those same adolescents may fail to perceive the connection between a rigorous grounding in mathematics and literature, and either their current or future lives. Perhaps Catholic education is the sort of experience that one is likely to look back upon with growing appreciation. Demanding teachers earn respect earlier than love, but both come in time for the good ones.

Concern for People

The simple between-group differences observed between Catholic high schools and public high schools on these variables were largely due to differences in the religiousness of the two groups of students; the regression analysis displayed relatively small school effects for the variables of *Make a Difference*, *Concern for Others*, and *Contribute Money*. In our model of Catholic school effects described below and represented in figure 3, we postulate a relationship between school and religiousness effects.

At-Risk Behaviors

This is an area in which previously persistent *School Type* differences disappeared, probably subsumed into *Nights Out*. We also note with some surprise the relatively modest impact of *Importance of Religion* in this area. Previous research (for major reviews, see Benson et al., 1989: Spilka et al., 1985) suggested that religion would be a much stronger inhibitor. We suspect that the problem in this instance is range restriction. Since a sample limited to Catholics is more religious, on average, than a sample of the general population, there is less variability in the religiousness measure within the Catholic student population in our study than was the case in other research.

Perceptions of Self

None of the concepts in this area were predicted very well by the background variables that were employed in these analyses. As we noted earlier, it may simply be the case that these "personality variables" are influenced largely by transient social conditions in the lives of high school seniors and do not vary consistently with the sorts of constructs that were examined in this survey.

Faith and Church

The remaining two areas in which we have observed a school effect are perhaps among the most impressive. *School Type* has a strong impact on the rated *Importance of Religion*; Catholic high school seniors rate religion as being more important to them than public high school seniors, even after background differences are taken into account. In addition, *School Type* influences *Church Attendance* over and above the separate influence of *Importance of Religion*. That is very impressive given the high correlation (.55) between those two variables in the general (i.e., Catholic and non-Catholic) sample. It indicates that Catholic high school attendance has a strong impact on this central aspect of Catholic church life.

Taken separately, *School Type* apparently does not predict either the desire to see the *Influence of Churches* increase in modern society or the likelihood that the student will make *Church Contributions* in future; to the extent that the variables we are using here can predict those two concepts, they are predicted solely by *Importance of Religion*. Of course, this finding may reflect an American Catholic perspective that focuses on the responsibility of individual Catholics to participate in the transformation of society through their own public and political efforts to promote gospel values (albeit consistent with the concerns of Catholic social teachings). In this view, it is the action of Catholics, rather than the influence of the institutional Church, that is seen as the priority.

A Model of Catholic High School Effects

The evidence gleaned from this re-examination of the *Monitoring the Future* data suggests that when non-academic school effects are found, they favor Catholic schools. This conclusion is suggested even though *Monitoring the Future* does not include measures of some of the value and behavior domains on which we would expect Catholic schools to do well. Instruction and formation in moral decision-making, sexual ethics, religious knowledge, Catholic orthodoxy, and global commitment are generally acknowledged as integral elements of the Catholic high school's mission, but these areas are, not surprisingly, excluded from the *Monitoring the Future* survey, which faces the same secular constraints as government funded schools.

Figure 3 portrays graphically what can now be said about the effects of Catholic school attendance. The solid lines reflect direct effects which have been demonstrated concerning three general sets of outcomes: academics; values, beliefs and behavior; and time use. The dotted lines represent what may be among the most important effects of Catholic education, and a fertile area for further research. They deal with what are two of the most important

FIGURE 3: The Effects of Attending Catholic High Schools

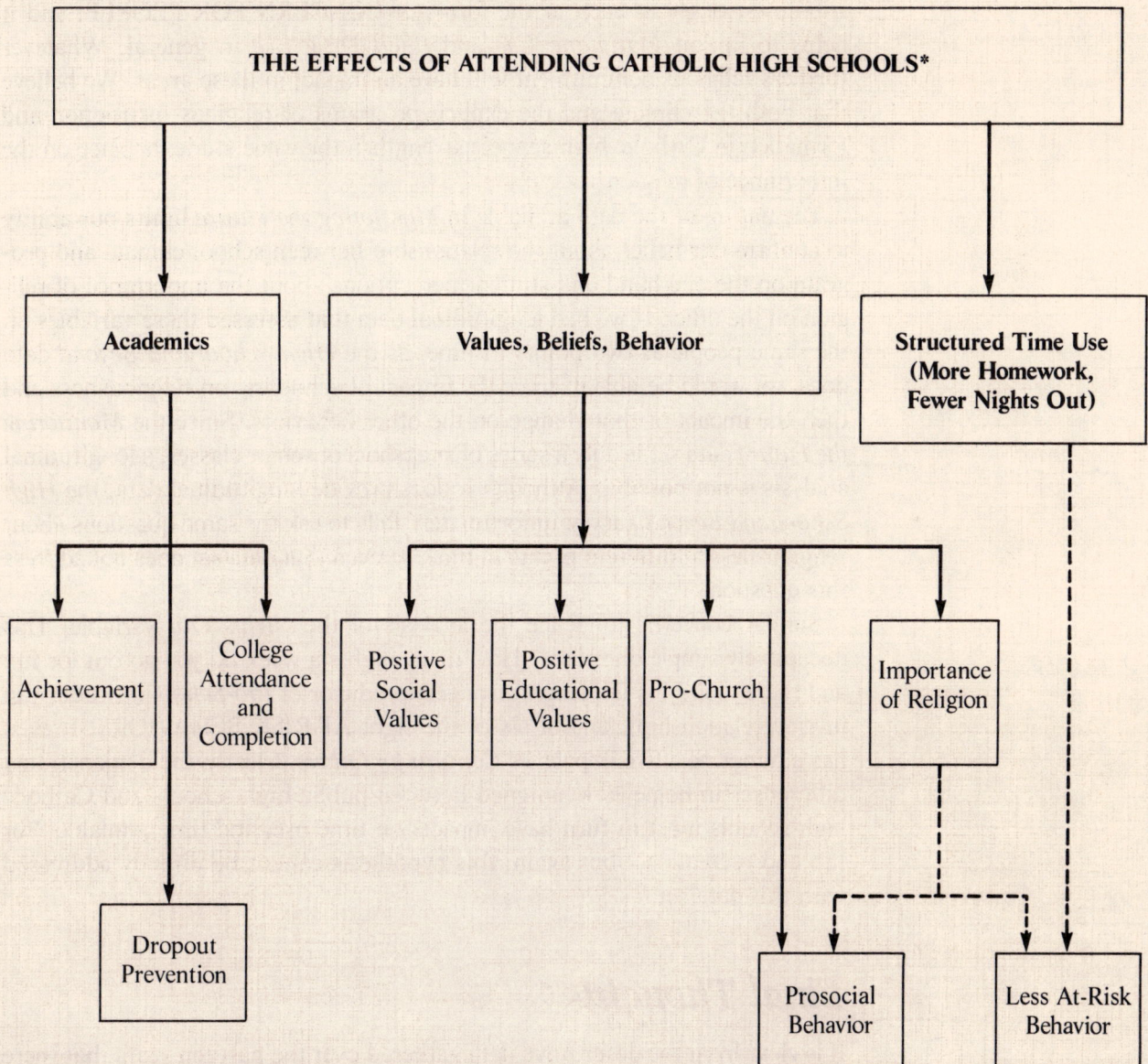

*Solid lines indicate empirically-demonstrated effects which favor Catholic high schools, in comparison to public high schools. Broken lines designate reasonable hypotheses about Catholic school effects which require additional confirmation.

effects of successful Catholic schools: the promotion of positive or "prosocial" behaviors, and the prevention of self-destructive or "at-risk" behaviors.

Of all the factors, the *Importance of Religion* is the strongest predictor of *Pro-Marriage* and *Pro-School* attitudes and *Community Involvement*. It contributes strongly to each of the forms of CONCERN FOR PEOPLE, and it helps to inhibit *Marijuana Use* and *Illicit Drug Use* in general. Whatever furthers religious commitment will have an impact in these areas. We believe that both the climate and the explicit programs of religious instruction and formation in Catholic high schools strengthen the value students place on the importance of religion.

The nature of the data available in *Monitoring the Future* limits our ability to confirm our belief about the relationship between school climate and program on the one hand and student perceptions about the importance of religion on the other. If we had longitudinal data that assessed these variables on the same people at two points in time, as the *High School and Beyond* data does, we would be able to trace the impact of schooling on religiousness and then the impact of that change on the other behaviors. Since the *Monitoring the Future* data set is only a series of snapshots of senior classes, a longitudinal analysis is not possible. Although it does provide longitudinal data, the *High School and Beyond* survey, unfortunately, fails to ask the same questions about religiousness at different points in time, so even that data set does not address this question.

Similar concerns influence the analysis of the *Nights Out* variable. This deceptively simple question, "How many nights a week do you go out for fun and recreation?" is the single strongest predictor of *Pro-School* attitudes (an inverse relationship), and of six of the eight AT-RISK BEHAVIORS. It even has a minor negative impact on *Concern for Others*. Clearly, the demonstrated differences in homework assigned between public high schools and Catholic high schools must in turn have impacts on time use, and time available "for fun and recreation," but again, this hypothesis cannot be directly addressed with this data set.

Final Thoughts

It is clear from the descriptive data gathered over the past ten years that there *are* significant value and behavior differences between Catholic seniors in Catholic high schools and those in public high schools. Where do they come from?

Some may suggest that they were there all along. They would argue that school choice is simply a reflection of a larger commitment to Catholic values on the part of both parent and child, and so the differences we observe in these seniors were present when they were freshman. But if these differences were pre-existing, we would expect them to be further associated with some of the family background variables we have discussed. Even when we control for those differences, school effects remain.

It seems eminently reasonable to assume that the factors that help to explain the positive academic effects of Catholic high schools are also at work in shaping non-academic outcomes. School climate, parental involvement, teacher commitment, strong school leadership, and the presence of a functional community may have an even stronger impact on the formation of student beliefs and values than they do on academic achievement. Certainly the presence of religious instruction within the academic program, and the opportunity to experience an examined and intellectually enriching faith in a setting open to the expression of religious feelings and helpful in dealing with religious doubt would enhance the development of a more mature faith. Opportunities for shared prayer and worship as well as institutional encouragement for service would also contribute to the unique spirit and vitality of Catholic high schools and their ability to influence the beliefs and values of their students.

Finally, however, the concept of the school as an integral element of a functional community must certainly be decisive. Unlike its public school counterpart, the Catholic high school is a part of a larger setting in which strength is drawn from a common moral language, a common history, and a shared vision of the human journey. While the concept itself may not be ideally suited to statistical measurement, it has been described in a variety of ways by a diverse group of authors and observers. Schools that are Catholic have roots that run deep. In the final analysis, Catholic schools are different, and they are successful, because they are Catholic.

Note

[1] A technical report prepared by Search Institute for the National Catholic Educational Association provides a detailed accounting of the statistical techniques employed in the analyses of these data. Scholars interested in the technical report may contact NCEA's Department of Secondary Schools. A few brief technical notes are presented here for the interested reader.

Differences between means in the "descriptive portrait" section were tested via a 2 (*Gender*) × 2 (*School Type*) general linear models analysis of variance. Because of the number of repeated tests and the unusually large sample size, differences are not reported as statistically significant unless $p < .0001$. Differences in the trend section were tested via a 3 (Period) × 2 (*Gender*) by 2 (*School Type*) analysis using the same specifications. Regression analyses employed a stepwise precedure that is invariant with respect to order of entry of the variables. Percent of explained variance for a given predictor is discussed only for predictor variables having partial R^2s of .01 or greater.

References

Alexander, K.L. (1987). Cross-section comparisons of public and private school effectiveness. A review of evidence and issues. In E.H. Haertel, T. James, and H.M. Levin (Eds.), *Comparing public and private schools: Volume 2. School achievement* (pp. 33-65). London: The Falmer Press

Argyle, M., and Beit-Hallahmi, B. (1975). *The social psychology of religion*. London: Routledge & Kegan Paul.

Benson, P.L., Donahue, M.J., and Erickson, J.A. (1989). Adolescence and religion: A review of the literature from 1970 to 1986. *Research in the Social Scientific Study of Religion*, 151-179.

Benson, P.L., and Guerra, M.J. (1985). *Sharing the faith: The beliefs and values of Catholic high school teachers*. Washington, DC: National Catholic Educational Association.

Benson, P.L., Yeager, R.J., Wood, P.K., Guerra, M.J., and Manno, B.V. (1986). *Catholic high schools: Their impact on low-income students*. Washington, DC: National Catholic Educational Association.

Bryk, A. (1988). Musings on the moral life of schools. *American Journal of Education, 96*, 274-275.

Chubb, J.E., and Moe, T.M. (1986). *Politics, markets, and the organization of schools*. Governmental Studies Discussion Paper #1. Washington, DC: The Brookings Institution.

Convey, J.J. (1984, May). Encouraging findings about students' religious values. *Momentum*, pp. 47-49.

Coleman, J.S., Hoffer, T. (1987). *Public and private high schools: The impact of communities*. New York: Basic Books.

Coleman, J.S., Hoffer, T., and Killgore, S. (1982). *High school achievement: Public, Catholic, and private schools compared*. New York: Basic Books.

Greeley, A. (1982). *Minority students in Catholic high schools*. New Brunswick, NJ: Transaction Books.

Greeley, A.M., McCready, W.C., and McCourt, K. (1976). *Catholic schools in a declining Church*. Mission, KS: Sheed and Ward.

Greeley, A.M., and Rossi, P.H. (1966). *The education of Catholic Americans*. Chicago: Aldine Publishing Company.

Fee, J.L., Greeley, A.M., McCready, W.C., and Sullivan, T.A. (1981). *Young Catholics: A report to the Knights of Columbus*. Los Angeles: Sadlier.

Haertel, E.H. (1987). Comparing public and private schools using longitudinal data from the HSB [High School and Beyond] study. In E.H. Haertel, T. James, and H.M. Levin (Eds.), *Comparing public and private schools: Volume 2. School achievement* (pp.9-32). London: The Falmer Press.

Haertel, E.H., James, T., and Levin, H.M. (Eds.) (1987a). *Comparing public and private schools: Volume 2. School achievement.* London: The Falmer Press.

Haertel, E.H., James, T., and Levin, H.M. (1987b). Introduction. In E.H. Haertel, T. James, and H.M. Levin (Eds.), *Comparing public and private schools: Volume 2. School achievement* (pp. 1-8). London: The Falmer Press.

Hoffer, T., Greeley, A.M., and Coleman, J.S. (1987). Catholic high school effects on achievement growth. In E.H. Haertel, T. James, and H.M. Levin (Eds.), *Comparing public and private schools: Volume 2. School achievement* (pp.67-88). London: The Falmer Press.

Johnston, L.D., Bachman, J.G., and O'Malley, P.M. (1986). *Monitoring the future: Questionnaire responses for the nation's high school seniors, 1985.* Ann Arbor: University of Michigan, Institute for Social Research.

Lee, V. (1985). *National assessment of educational progress, reading proficiency: 1983-84: Catholic school results and national averages.* Washington, DC: National Catholic Educational Association.

Lee, V., and Stewart, C. (1989, March 29). [Interview] *USA Today,* p. D-1.

A nation at risk: The imperative for educational reform: An open letter to the American people. (1983, April) Washington, DC: National Commission on Excellence in Education.

National Conference of Catholic Bishops. (1983). *The challenge of peace: God's promise and our response: A pastoral letter on war and peace.* Washington, DC: United States Catholic Conference.

Occhiogrosso, P. (1987). *Once a Catholic: Prominent Catholics and ex-Catholics reveal the influence of the Church on their lives and work.* Boston: Houghton Mifflin.

Spilka, B., Hood, R.W., Jr., and Gorsuch, R.L. (1985). *The psychology of religion: An empirical approach.* Englewood Cliffs, NJ: Prentice Hall.

Walberg, H.J., and Shanahan, T. (1983). High school effects on individual students. *Educational Researcher, 12*(7), 4-9.

Walberg, H.J., Bakalis, M.J., Bast, J.L., and Baer, S. (1988). *We can rescue our children: The cure for Chicago's public school crisis—with lessons for the rest of America.* Chicago: The Heartland Institute.

What works: Research about teaching and learning. (1986). Washington, DC: United States Department of Education.